inCourage

STRENGTHENED FROM WITHIN

By: Arletha S. Kent

Arletha Kent

This is Your Season!

To: Charlene

Self-Published - Arletha S. Kent

Limits of Liability-Disclaimer
The author and publisher shall not be liable for your misuse of this material. The purpose of this book is to educate and entertain. The author or publisher does not guarantee that anyone following these techniques, suggestions, tips, ideas, or strategies will become successful. The author or publisher shall have neither liability nor responsibility to anyone with respect to any loss of, damage caused, or alleged to be caused, directly or indirectly by the information contained in this book.

Photography: Cedric Scott Photography

Cover: Michael Tarrell Full Media Design

Book Formatting: Joy E. Turner, JetSet Communications & Consulting

Hair Stylist: LaShelle Gooch

Make-up & Wardrobe: Arletha S. Kent

Website Design: Arletha S. Kent

Ministry Flyer Design: Stephanie Smith - Touch of Class Studio & Graphix

ISBN 978-0-692-60082-5
Library of Congress 1-2963162891

Printed in USA by Publishers Graphics Commercial Letter USA

www.arlethakentministries.org

Table of Contents

Foreword

"*inCourage*" Prophetess Arletha Kent

It is such a pleasure to read in this season, something so refreshing, as well as informative, to the Body of Christ, *inCourage: Strengthened from Within*, by Prophetess Arletha Kent. I have had the privilege to work with her on several occasions and am so grateful to the LORD to see her and the ministry entrusted into her hands, grow and develop to bring glory to GOD.

Each chapter challenges us to take a personal assessment in areas of our lives, which GOD may desire to enhance.

One of my favorite chapters, "Purpose is Power", resonates with a distinct admonishment to the Body of Christ to operate in purpose on a daily basis.

This anointed woman of GOD has so adequately articulated the importance of grasping the revelation and realization, that our lives have purpose. The more that we are "*inCourage*" the better we are able to "encourage" others. What we possess on the inside of us can be used to equip and empower those around us. The Scripture tells us in 1 Sam. 30:6 but David encouraged himself in the LORD his GOD.

"What you believe dictates your decisions," is definitely an eye-opening chapter. Whatever we believe and act upon directly affects our destiny. Arletha points us to GOD, His Spirit and His word, to lead and guide us in every aspect of our life.

Prophetess Kent has provided us with valuable tools to help us walk out our GOD given destiny, not only purpose driven but Power infused. It gives us a simple approach to obtaining and maintaining a continuously victorious mindset. Her passion is for those, who are willing to be all that GOD intended for them to be in this season, and to enjoy the journey. What better way for it to be expressed than by someone who has actually experienced it.

This book gives us a simple approach. Readers, this book will challenge you to move forward, not backward, and finish strong "*inCourage!*"

Apostle Barbara J. McClain

Barbara McClain Ministries – Kingdom International Institute, St. Louis, MO.
"Training and Equipping Kingdom People for the End-Times"

Introduction

InCourage: Strengthened From Within has been tailor made just for you! As God reveals to you the intentions of His heart, I pray that you embrace the love of God and allow yourself to be healed from the inside out. God wants to complete what He has started in your life, but it will require your cooperation and participation.

The Goal here is for you to discover, through the Holy Spirit, what are your gifts, talents, and calling. The ultimate outcome is for you to walk in liberty and possess your authority as a kingdom citizen! This instructional book has been designed for you to strategically dig into the dark places of your life that you may have forgotten about or just never had the courage to face, which have hindered you from walking in the fullness of God.

The Holy Spirit has formulated questions and solutions to address what you have been dealing with. I am excited for you and pray that you receive and maintain your deliverance once and for all!

1

"WHAT YOU BELIEVE"

DICTATES YOUR DECISIONS

Chapter 1

"Have I not commanded you? Be strong and of good courage; do not be afraid, nor be dismayed, for the Lord your God is with you wherever you go."

- Joshua 1:9

There's an old saying that goes "a guarantee is only as good as the guarantor." Our ability to believe what someone says to us is most of the time based on the track record of the person who's saying it. But what if that "someone" is God who said it? Unfortunately, we sometimes can be a people who allow the betrayal of our trust by other people to cause us to become suspect of God. We may have experienced things that at one time or another, we believed it was the right thing to do, place to be or person to trust. Later we found ourselves regretting putting our trust in them and making those decisions and now we're afraid of believing anything else for fear of being disappointed again.

Well, the only problem with that is, when we say we won't put our trust in anyone else again doesn't mean that our desires to be better and do better is just going to go away. Look, I want to bring something to your attention. Have you ever taken the time to evaluate what you believe? I mean really take the time to see and dig deep into why you believe what you believe? Did you know that to really believe something or someone, there has to be some sort of action to follow that makes a statement that you believe what you say you believe? So in essence, what we believe really should dictate our decisions. And in many of our instances, they did. The issue was that a lot of the decisions we made in times past were based on what we were "believing" at the time that we didn't know, we shouldn't have been "believing." Well thanks be unto God, He is going to show us through this book and by His Spirit that what we should be believing in is His word and His ability to bring His promises to pass concerning us.

So what do we do with these desires the Lord has placed on the inside of us? Well, first things first, we must take heed to the command that the Lord gave Joshua when He told him to "Be strong and of good courage." Our ability to believe God and take Him at His word is going to be key for us. Unlike Joshua, who was told to *"be of good courage,"* we have a better advantage than he did. Our courage comes from the fact that the One who supplies us with the courage is on the inside of us! Yes, our New Testament covenant states that it is *"Christ in us the hope of glory"* (Colossians 1:27). So because of the fact that we are "in Christ" gives us the winning edge against any situations or problems that can arise in our lives because Christ is on the inside of us providing strength and courage to carry out our assignments in the earth.

In: Expressing the situation of being enclosed or surrounded by something.

Courage: The quality of mind or spirit that enables a person to face difficulty, danger, pain, etc., without fear.

This is where the revelation of "*inCourage*" came from. As we function in the capacity of who Christ is in us and not in our strength and abilities, it minimizes or eliminates the doubts and fears that come to hinder us. Our limits and hang-ups are totally a non-factor in the matter when our assurance in Christ is in full effect. The Father wants us to get free from the hurts and wounds of the past and move forward "*inCourage*" to accomplish the purpose and plans He has for our lives. So as we go on from this point, just know that to be "*inCourage*" for the believer is to be "in Christ." Now, let's deal with what's on the inside of you that you've been suppressing…

There comes a time when enough has to be enough! You know that time has come, because what's on the inside of you is ready to erupt like a volcano.

I'm talking about nights when you can't sleep because all you can think about is your dreams, visions, and aspirations. This includes the days you can't concentrate or focus because you're frustrated and don't know why.

This brings you to the point when you realize you have no business where you are; whether it's that unhealthy relationship that's costing you everything, that house you shouldn't have bought, that job you settled for, that emotional decision that caused you to make a commitment to someone or something that is only weighing you down, or that opportunity you let pass you by for one reason or another. Whatever the issue may be, you're ready to make some changes NOW!

You're at a crossroad where everything in you longs to come out, be it your gifts, talents, entrepreneurship, ministry gifts, etc. But you either don't know where to start, don't ***believe*** it will ever happen, afraid of failure, afraid of success, worried about what people are going to think of you, or you keep putting other people before yourself, which won't allow you to accomplish anything. These distractions, and hindrances are designed to deter you from your destiny. I call these symptoms of the issue. Whatever the issue may be, these symptoms are the results of the decisions you made based on what you believed. And the enemy has used them to convince you of why you can't do what God is calling you to do.

The fact of the matter is, something led you to this place of discontentment. My goal here is to get you to realize that the issue and symptoms are not the source of what you're dealing with. Something is causing you to make poor decisions, compromise, settle, etc…To really know what that is, which I will refer to as the root cause, will require some serious soul-searching and self-assessments by way of the Holy

Spirit which will reveal the root cause of the issue. When you uproot the issue and allow the Holy Spirit to reveal the root cause of what's actually going on, you can, by the power of God's word, renew your mind and crucify your flesh and the symptoms will die. This is what I call your process of sanctification, which will enable you to walk in the fullness of God.

Sanctification: The process of being made holy resulting in a changed lifestyle for the believer.

When we submit to Him and commit to the process of sanctification, He can begin to mold, shape, and transform us into the image of His Son Jesus Christ (2 Thessalonians 2:13). In this place we feed our spirit on His word and starve our flesh, which will enable us to be transformed by the renewing of our minds (Romans 12:2). Here we are no longer ruled or controlled by our emotions.

The scripture says in 2 Thessalonians 2:13, "*But we are bound to give thanks always to God for you, brethren beloved of the Lord, because God hath from the beginning chosen you to salvation through sanctification of the Spirit and belief of the truth:*"

What we as Kingdom Citizens experience should be predicated upon what we believe. What we believe produces fruit whether good or bad. I've found that not all good intentions produce good fruit. This is why we must make certain that what we believe is in line with the word of God and is rightly divided (2 Timothy 2:15). I know that place oh so well…

The Lord wants us to be free from bondage holistically.

John 10:10 says, "*The thief comes only in order to steal and kill and destroy. I came that they may have and enjoy life, and have it in abundance (to the full, till it overflows).*" {Amp}

I really want you to understand what I mean by the sanctification process through self-assessment, so I have listed some of my results below. As you read this chapter, I want you to pray this prayer and ask the Holy Spirit to reveal to you the root cause of what you're experiencing so it can be dealt with once and for all!

EE PAPER

Shop 'n Save

10461 Manchester Road
Kirkwood, MO 63122
Store Phone # (314) 984-0322
Store Director: Eric

Cashier:Kadi C

07/11/16 14:19:27

MEAT
SB BF RND STK BNLS 25177200000 5.10 FT
0.73 lb @ 6.99 / lb
PRODUCE
PINK LADY APPLES 4130 .89 FT
DAIRY
EE CTG CHEESE SMAL 4130302499 2.99 FT
SUBTOTAL 8.98
5.225% Sales Tax .47
TOTAL 9.45
Cash TENDER 20.00
Cash CHANGE 10.55

NUMBER OF ITEMS 3

Trx:121 Oper 113 Term: 9 Store: 1816
07/11/16 14:19:43

Low prices. Every day!
****
Pharmacy Phone # (314) 984-0422

www.shopnsave.com

Enter to be a weekly winner

of a $100 gift card!!

Go to: www.shopnsavelistens.com

Code: 07111 81650 090121

Take the survey within 3 days

****

RE!
L 855-275-7010
R DETAILS
rtui
Register Tapes Unlimited, L.P.
www.rtui.com
DOES REGISTER TAPE
ADVERTISING
WORK?
it just did!
FOR INFORMATION CALL
855-275-7010
rtui
Make The Right Move...
Register Tape
Advertising
Works!
855-275-7010
ATTENTION CASHIERS: START THIS TAPE 6/20/16 RTUI, L.P. ©2016
PLAY IT AGAIN SPORTS®
Your Neighborhood
Sporting Goods Store
REUSE. RECYCLE. REPLAY.®
SH01816JJA
15% OFF Any Purchase
Cannot be used with other discounts or offers, or all ready discounted items.
Maximum discount of $20.00. With coupon. Expires 10/15/16.
10947 Manchester Road • Kirkwood • 314-821-4567
DOWNLOAD
RTUI's Free
Coupon App
rtui.com
Register Tapes Unlimited, L.P.
App Store
SAVE

Prayer

Father God, in the name of Jesus,

Thank you for the gift of repentance, grace and mercy that allows me to make the necessary changes to be ready and available to you. I repent Father in the name of Jesus for allowing my feelings and emotions to pull me out of your presence. Here I am Lord, ready to commune with you. Holy Spirit speak to my heart. Show me the path to righteousness. Show me the errors of my ways that I may be pleasing in Your sight.

In Jesus' name Amen...

The assessment is broken down into 3 integral parts: the issue, the symptom, and the root cause. As you acknowledge the issue, identify the symptom, and allow the Holy Spirit to reveal the root cause, then God can heal and restore you!

Here are some of the questions I had to ask myself that lead me to BELIEVE I was doing the right thing or making the right decision along with my answers, which I will refer to as the issue and symptom. The revelation from the Holy Spirit will be referred to as the root cause:

1. **What do you "believe" you need to be complete or happy?**

____

____

____

____

____

____

____

____

My Answer / Issue: I believed a loving family and true friends were what I needed to be happy and complete.

Symptoms: What I needed was someone to love, support, and understand me. Since it seemed no one wanted to give me any of these, I became very sad, insecure, suicidal, and defensive and the list goes on.

Revelation/ Root Cause: I experienced constant rejection in times past. I was always complete in Christ Jesus. What I was longing for was always there. I didn't realize how much God loved me. I didn't know how to allow His word to support me and I didn't think about how He created me and that He knows everything about me. I was taught who He was but not who I was to Him.

2. What do you want to accomplish in the near future?

____

____

____

____

____

____

My Answer/ Issue: All I wanted to do was assist with the growth and development of others. This included anyone with ambitions. I wanted to open a community center with various resources, I became a foster parent, a godmother to countless children, I was a Program Director for a non–profit organization, and I developed different self-developmental groups and workshops throughout my community and city. This is all I wanted to do.

Symptoms: I experienced major anxiety, a lot of sleepless nights, lawless giving, and sometimes putting myself in harmful situations.

Revelation/ Root Cause: Self-gratification. I was governing myself. Everything I wanted to do was unknowingly motivated by what I believed I was missing in my life. Instead of being led by the Holy Spirit to do as God willed, I was doing everything I needed to do to create a sense of self-value. Helping others created an environment that would let them see I loved them in hope that they would love me back. I wanted them to see I was there for them and that they were like family to me. I created a false reality.

I learned that every good and perfect gift that was invested in me should have been used for God's glory and governed by the Holy Spirit. I **believed** what I felt in my heart was just the type of person I was.

I didn't know, the Holy Spirit, through the motivational gifts (which are the Gifts of prophecy, serving, teaching, exhorting, giving, organizing and mercy as found in Romans 12:4-8,) given to all believers to demonstrate Gods love and power to the church and to the world, was in operation, but because I wasn't acquainted with Him (Holy Spirt), I attributed my actions to my person.

As I began to seek God, He revealed to me that satan had been manipulating me and I was misappropriating the gifts which drained me and caused me to wander from the will of God. I pray that you find yourself in some of the motivational gifts, which will help you accept that God created you the way you are on purpose. I want you to forgive yourself and stop apologizing for being you and ask God to teach you how to be the best you that you can be. Satan knew I wasn't aware of what was on the inside of me and he did his best to make sure I never found out…**But God!**

As I expose the enemy, I'm going to show you I was being my authentic self, but not knowing who I was to God, caused ME some issues. As I said earlier, I was taught who God was, but not who I was to God…

These are some of the motivational gifts that I was operating in but was not aware:

Gift of Prophecy: it exposes and encourages. I would see things and know things about specific people and situations that always seemed to happen just as it was revealed to me. I would say "Something told me or I knew that was going to happen." So I'd do everything in my power to help the person try to avoid the bad things that I saw and also, try to help them accomplish the good things I saw.

I didn't understand that there was a prophetic call on my life and that God was showing me things so He could accomplish His purpose in the situation through prayer. Instead of me responding by way of prayer, I responded out of my emotions, feeling obligated to fix the problem myself, because I knew how it felt to need someone to care and help. **I didn't know the purpose and power of prayer.**

Gift of Serving: Demonstrates love by meeting the needs of others. It was natural for me to be the first one to volunteer. I believed I just loved helping people. The fact of the matter was, I did love helping people, but I had to learn how to gage my discernment and hear from the Holy Spirit to get permission to help the person and instructions on how to help them.

There were times He wanted me to help someone with food. I would automatically go buy bags and bags of groceries, but He only wanted me to buy a meal because He had plans for how they would get the second meal, which would accomplish His purpose and reveal His glory in their situation.

I learned that receiving a vision without instructions can be dangerous for all parties involved. For the receiver, they didn't have to rely on God because I played God for them. This in some instances caused the person to have to remain in that place until God was able to do what He wanted to do in their life.

And for me, I experienced a lot of heartache because the person didn't appreciate or recognize the sacrifice I made which caused me to feel like I wasted my time and money. These are called false assignments.

Gift of Teaching: Teachers have the duty of instructing and instilling kingdom principles that help the believer apply the word of God to their daily life. My goal was to make sure those around me understood they could accomplish anything they put their minds to. It was important that they knew there was a solution to the problem. Use the solution and move on.

I learned that everyone has a due season. I would stress myself out when those I loved continued to remain in unhealthy situations. I wanted them to get it so bad that I found myself saying the right thing at the wrong time. I learned that God will release a word to me that was not for me to release to the other person at that time. He knows where they are and all I knew is where I wanted them to be.

Exhorting: Encourages and uplifts others, shares wisdom and gives Godly counsel. I always had a heart for the "underdog." Strangers would just open up to me and I found myself giving advice.

In situations like this, I would go out on a limb for people. I would sacrifice my time to make sure everything was in place for the person to get a running start because again, I knew what it was like to be driven to accomplish something and no one cared enough to invest time into me becoming the best I could be.

I learned the hard way that some people operate in motivation and not determination. Those people that are motivated must be motivated over and over and as a result, they will drain and distract you from what God has called you to do.

Determined people can't rest until they get out what is in them. They take the given advice and apply it. They utilize resources. If you show them, they will run with it! The person operating in the gift of Exhorting, must be lead by the Holy Spirit. The one operating by merely wanting to help others is being led by emotions. Being led by the Holy Spirit protects us from spinning our wheels.

Giving: Ready and willing to meet the needs of others. I never get attached to anything. There is nothing I own even to this day that I couldn't give away at the drop of a hat.

Here is where I used to get in the most trouble. I would give things away that I had been blessed with. I didn't consider the fact that God moved in those areas concerning my needs. I would give without seeking God for permission, giving my blessings away. Some things I had been given were for me to enjoy. I would give out of season and found myself sowing into bad ground. Sometimes, I never received a harvest on what I gave, but instead, had to "GROW THROUGH" that season to a place of wisdom for the next opportunity to properly give. I had to wait until He blessed me again. I must say, instead of me enjoying the blessing of God, I had to experience being kept. He wanted me blessed not just kept!

Organizing: Carries out projects by recruiting workers, organizing tasks, or delegating responsibilities. I have always been a leader of some sort. I recognized this at an early age. I was the person that if you wanted it done right call me. I'm not saying this in a boastful way, but it's the truth. I somehow always made things happen that others couldn't.

God would give me a vision and instead of me waiting on specific instructions, I would run, create a blue print and find people to assist me.

Now here is the hard truth! In this, I found myself always frustrated because it seemed like the help would be working against me instead of with me. This would hurt my heart so bad. My abilities seemed to annoy them. I remember asking myself "What is the problem and why did they agree to help me?" As I said before, I didn't know the Holy Spirit in the way I do now, but it was Him allowing me to discern envy and jealousy. He showed me the enemy's plan to sabotage the vision. One day the Holy Spirit said, "What if Noah received the vision to build the Ark and didn't get detailed instructions (Genesis 6:13 22) on specific wood, exact measurements and who was supposed to be onboard?" I can't imagine the damage of Noah having the bright idea to add an extra deck or extra window. We would still be affected by that to this day. But instead we are living in the blessings of His obedience.

Mercy: Demonstrates God's love and compassion. I have always had a heart for people less fortunate and abused. It's second nature for me to find a solution to problems.

I had to learn the difference between empathy and sympathy. They both have their place. Not knowing when to apply them properly can be dangerous.

1) Empathy: The ability to understand and share the feelings of another.

2) Sympathy: a feeling of support for something.

Mixing these two up cost me a lot of money, time and heartache. The enemy knows you have this gift, so he will make sure individuals make their way to you.

An example of this is someone who may or may not ask, but needs resources for whatever reason. It is important to seek God on how to respond instead of reacting. You must know if anything comes up and causes you to shift directions to do or go opposite of where you were originally instructed from the Holy Spirit, this could be a trick of the enemy to lure you off to dangerous ground mentally, emotionally, or spiritually.

I have heard of men and women of God losing their lives by opening up their homes to the enemy because someone needed a place to stay. They felt compassion for them, but didn't ask God for permission to allow the person to stay and the enemy was on assignment to take their life.

We must not allow our emotions to get the best of us. Being emotional is like being intoxicated because you cannot make any rational or wise decisions.

We must ask God for Wisdom in all we do (James 1:5). *1 Corinthians 12:11 says, "But one and the same Spirit works all these things, distributing to each one individually as He wills."*

To sum it all up God has placed all these gifts in us by His spirit to benefit us all, but as I have learned, we must make sure that we are operating in them as the Holy Spirit wills and not as *we* will.

3. Who or what do you "believe" is preventing you from accomplishing your goals?

____

____

____

____

____

____

My Answer/ Issue: I was preventing myself from accomplishing my goals. I took on responsibilities that would not financially allow me to invest in my projects due to my responsibilities and obligation to other people.

Symptoms: Frustration, aggravation, shame, etc...

Revelation/ Root Cause: Abandonment... The Lord had major doors open for me that I allowed to close because of my emotional decisions. It was never His will for me to struggle by taking on the cares of the world and seeking love and approval from others. ***This caused me to operate in the spirit of pride. Yes! I said the spirit of pride…I will explain later in this chapter.***

4. How did "who" or "what" become a hindrance to you accomplishing your goals?

____

____

____

____

____

My Answer/Issue: I was the hindrance, because I surrounded myself with people completely opposite of me. I'm speaking of the drive and determination I had. I voluntarily assumed responsibility for things they needed because I believed I was called to do it. Never seeking God for direction, instead I made emotional decisions.

Symptoms: Frustration and anxiety.

Revelation/ Root Cause: I became an enabler.

The opportunities for me to be a blessing to others required me getting specific instructions on how, when and where to be a blessing so I could allow God to be God in their lives.

Enabler: *one that enables another to achieve an end; to make able; give power, means, competence, or ability to; authorize: to make possible or easy.*

5. What were you thinking or feeling when you allowed who or what in your life?

____

____

____

____

____

My Answer/ Issue: All I focused on was making sure others never experienced what I experienced which was rejection, lack of support, low self-esteem, never being good enough, and the list goes on.

Symptoms: I never had time for me, I was stressed, developed acid reflux and experienced many sleepless nights.

Revelation/ Root Cause: Also stemmed from self-gratification and rejection…I needed to be healed from things in my past that I didn't know were there. There were spirits assigned to me as a young child. I remembered being frustrated, sad and angry a lot. I would be on the side of the house where no one could see me and would take my fist and rub it against the bricks on the house as I walked and cried until my knuckles bled. Through different hurts and disappointments I formed an opinion of how life was going to be when I grew up. *A lot of those acts of kindness was me unknowingly filling voids that were in my life which caused me to love selfishly. Yes! I said love selfishly... All this was designed to deter me from my true calling, purpose and destiny.*

6. What were you thinking at the time who or what became a consideration of commitment?

____

____

____

____

My Answer/ Issue: I wanted to hold on to what made me feel safe. I wanted to focus on what I was good at that allowed me to see some results of my hard work. It gave me a sense of accomplishment. I wanted to create an environment that fostered all the things I was missing and deprived of.

Symptoms: Stress, Confrontation from different sources, tension in other relationships including my marriage, etc.

Revelation/RootCause: Also stemmed from rejection…I learned that the steps of a righteous man are ordered by the Lord and that God is a God of order and purpose. My peace was only found in Him. It was not His will for me to endure some of the hardships I created for myself. All good ideas and deeds are not inspired by the Holy Spirit! Some of the decisions I made were not wise. I'm still recovering from some of them to this day. I thank God for grace and mercy.

"Good Intentions don't always produce Good fruit"

In your observation, do you see how in my mind, (which was what I BELIEVED), I was doing the right thing? While all along I was operating out of a place of hurt that caused me to adapt to a *coping mechanism.*

Coping mechanism: An adaptation to environmental stress that is based on conscious or unconscious choices and that enhances control over behavior or gives psychological comfort.

I found a way to function in the midst of dysfunction. I convinced myself, by giving tirelessly to those in need, it would pay off one day. At the same time, in my mind, I believed I would never be loved the way I loved. So as long as I did my best at being what others needed me to be, that was enough for me. I learned how to take the pain and disappointments and use them as a reason to isolate myself mentally and emotionally. I was always around a lot of people, but very much alone. I would focus on different projects or endeavors that took me away from the issues that were going on around me and from the hurt and pain that I was carrying. Due to some major blows that I experienced, I became very angry and frustrated for a season.

Being a person that only wanted to love, I prayed, ***BELIEVING*** I got past the anger and frustration. I even forgave some people. After all of that, I noticed, depending on the situation, I had developed triggers that caused me to react out of my emotions based on past hurts or disappointments.

In this, I figured out different ways I could keep my heart and mind safe. This made me feel I had some control of my feelings, emotions and space. This is what I meant by I opened myself up to the spirit of pride.

Pride: A sense of one's own proper dignity or value; self-respect.

The strategies the enemy presented to me were all bricks that I used to build a wall between God and me. I "believed" I had to protect myself. It seemed like this was the time new people would come into my space trying to get close, but I couldn't receive it because I didn't want to get hurt. (Chuckle) God started to send the very thing I longed for, but I couldn't recognize it. I viewed it as the devil trying to set me up.

The spirit of pride is very deceiving. Proverbs 11:2 says, *"When swelling and pride come, then emptiness and shame come also, but with the humble (those who are lowly, who have been pruned or chiseled by trial, and renounce self) are skillful and godly wisdom and soundness."* {Amp}

People only look at pride in the sense of being arrogant or puffed up. But the spirit of pride is in operation, when you think you can take better care of yourself than God. When you have the answer to the problem that is outside of what the Lord is telling you to do. The spirit of pride will overtake you. It will cause you to react to things by worldly principles instead of responding with the word according to the principles of God.

1 John 2:16 says: *"For all that is in the world the lust of the flesh [craving for sensual gratification] and the lust of the eyes [greedy longings of the mind] and the pride of life [assurance in one's own resources or in the stability of earthly things]—these do not come from the Father but are from the world [itself]."* {Amp}

<u>BUT!</u>

James 4:6 says: *"But He gives us more and more grace"* (power of the Holy Spirit, to meet this evil tendency and all others fully.) That is why He says, God sets Himself against the proud and haughty, but gives grace [continually] to the lowly (those who are humble enough to receive it). {Amp}

This spirit of pride distorts perception. It always tracks back to the following:

- ✓ ***I think***
- ✓ ***I feel***
- ✓ ***I want***
- ✓ ***I need***
- ✓ ***I'm Gonna***
- ✓ ***I'm not***
- ✓ ***I can't***

One of the deceptions of this spirit is:

Manipulation: It manipulates you by magnifying what's important to you and it gives you its own priority list. It always puts kingdom principles last. It has a way of promoting religion, tradition and the world's way of doing things at the same time.

You know it's in operation when you're doing everything your mind tells you to do, but afterwards you are still miserable, disappointed, depressed, angry, discontent, etc.

You may even achieve some of your goals concerning education, purchasing your new home or car, your career, or companionship, but realize something is still missing.

Everything you have obtained seems to be working against you or just not profitable. You have to work hard to keep it or them. It seems like peace is so far out of your reach. You realize you are never fulfilled…The truth is, only what we do in Christ will last. There is no peace outside of the will of God.

John 16:33 says, *"I have told you these things, so that in Me you may have [perfect] peace and confidence. In the world you have tribulation and trials and distress and frustration; but be of good cheer [take courage; be confident, certain, undaunted]! For I have overcome the world. [I have deprived it of power to harm you and have conquered it for you.]"* {AMP}

Now, the fact is, I'm a woman of many talents, gifts, and skills that some have confessed to admire and envy. I have been called upon by people older than I for advice because of the wisdom that I possess at a young age. I am the one everyone calls if they want something done and done right. All the while struggling within myself and at the time, unaware of what I was dealing with. I loved God and wanted Him to be pleased with me. The missing element was relationship. I didn't know Him, I knew about Him.

It was upon me learning the nature and character of God that I was able to embrace what I "believed" His word said about me. I began to study the word of God to see His view on some of the things I felt and struggled with. I accepted my healing by:

1. **Embracing the idea that God wants what's best for me and He loves me. He died for me which makes me worth it!**

   Jeremiah 29:11…"*For I know the thoughts and plans that I have for you, says the Lord, thoughts and plans for welfare and peace and not for evil, to give you hope in your final outcome.*" {Amp}

2. **Fully forgiving and releasing everyone who hurt me.**

   Ephesians 4:32 "*and be kind to one another, tenderhearted, forgiving one another, even as God in Christ forgave you.*"

3. **Allowing the Holy Spirit to condition my heart which changed my mind set.**

   Romans 12:2…"*Do not be conformed to this world (this age), [fashioned after and adapted to its external, superficial customs], but be transformed (changed) by the [entire] renewal of your mind [by its new ideals and its new attitude], so that you may prove [for yourselves] what is the good and acceptable and perfect will of God, even the thing which is good and acceptable and perfect [in His sight for you].*" {AMP}

4. Learning how to trust Him with me.

> Proverbs 3:5…"*Lean on, trust in, and be confident in the Lord with all your heart and mind and do not rely on your own insight or understanding.* {AMP}
>
> Romans 8:28…"*We are assured and know that God being a partner in their labor] all things work together and are [fitting into a plan] for good to and for those who love God and are called according to [His] design and purpose.*"

This was my road to success. Not what I accomplished and achieved through worldly principles, but how successful I was with hearing and obeying the voice of the Lord.

Joshua 1:6-9 says, "*Be strong (confident) and of good courage, for you shall cause this people to inherit the land which I swore to their fathers to give them. Only you be strong and very courageous, that you may do according to all the law which Moses my servant commanded you. Turn not from it to the right hand or to the left that you may prosper wherever you go. This Book of the Law shall not depart out of your mouth, but you shall meditate on it day and night, that you may observe and do according to all that is written in it. For then you shall make your way prosperous, and then you shall deal wisely and have good success. Have not I commanded you? Be strong, vigorous, and very courageous. Be not afraid, neither be dismayed, for the Lord your God is with you wherever you go.*"

At this point I was able to allow what I believed to dictate my decisions and it produced good fruit… John 15: says: *"When you bear (produce) much fruit, My Father is honored and glorified, and you show and prove yourselves to be true followers of Mine."* {AMP}

Believe: a: to consider to be true or honest
b: to accept the word or evidence of

When what you believe starts to affect your decisions, you can no longer carry on opposite of what you know and feel in your spirit. If you believe what God has spoken to you through His spirit, through His word or through His prophet, you will begin to position yourself for manifestation.

If you believe in what God has invested in you, there is outward evidence that will display through your actions. You begin to strengthen yourself in those areas through different trainings i.e., classes, research, networking. This is when you step out on faith and operate in the confidence of who Jesus Christ is and what He has done and not in your skills, abilities and strength. This takes much prayer for direction and guidance by way of the Holy Spirit.

When what you believe affects your decisions, you're not easily manipulated, seduced, distracted, offended, or intimidated. In this place you never make emotional decisions but rather operate in wisdom.

Wisdom allows you to respond to situations and circumstances appropriately and not emotionally.

You respond knowing what's best for you and not by what you want, knowing in your heart it's not in line with what God has purposed for your life.

What you believe should be your way of living. Your morals should be based on what you believe. The principles you stand by should be in line with what you believe according to the word of God.

Let's take your name for instance. You know your name and there is nothing anyone can say or do to make you think otherwise. If someone stood in your face and told you your name was Brenda instead of Karen you would probably look at them crazy and laugh at them. After a while you may get a little annoyed and then dismiss yourself out of the conversation. There is only so far that conversation would go before you come to the conclusion it's pointless to argue about something you already know.

In conclusion to this chapter, stand on what you believe no matter what it looks like or feels like and trust God when it comes to you. Invest your time in what He has invested in you by learning who you are, what your gifts and talents are. Believe in who He says you are, embracing who you are and being determined to operate in your full potential by casting down fear, anxiety, doubt, insecurities, unforgiveness and operate in confidence, boldness, peace, forgiveness and most of all LOVE!

2

“PERCEPTION IS KEY”

WHAT PROVOKES YOUR BEHAVIOR?

Chapter 2

In this chapter, we're going to focus on your self-perception.

Perception: the way you think about or understand someone or something.

Before you can be anything to anyone else, you have to know and love the real you. Not the "you" your family genetics say you are. Not the "you" bad things happened to. Not the "you" no one seems to love. But "you," who God created in His likeness and His image!

Genesis 1:26-27 says: *"God said, Let Us [Father, Son, and Holy Spirit] make mankind in Our image, after Our likeness, and let them have complete authority over the fish of the sea, the birds of the air, the [tame] beasts, and over all of the earth, and over everything that creeps upon the earth.So God created man in His own image, in the image and likeness of God He created him; male and female He created them."*

Ephesians 1:4-5 says: *"Even as [in His love] He chose us [actually picked us out for Himself as His own] in Christ before the foundation of the world, that we should be holy (consecrated and set apart for Him) and blameless in His sight, even above reproach, before Him in love. For He foreordained us (destined us, planned in love for us) to be adopted (revealed) as His own children through Jesus Christ, in accordance with the purpose of His will because it pleased Him and was His kind intent."* {AMP}

Before we go into our perception of who we think we are, let's talk about the truth of God's word concerning us. We see that in Genesis 1, we are made in His image and likeness, which is our spirit man. Every bit of dominion He gave us was to that man. Our ability to be successful was already placed on the inside of us and it is from our spirit man that we were designed to make decisions for our life. However, despite the fall of man, God already had a plan to redeem us back to a place of power by sending His Son Jesus to enable us to carry out His purpose (Ephesians 1:4-5).

Satan, our adversary, is a master manipulator when it comes to taking things from the elements around us and causing us to perceive things differently than we should. He has been doing this since the garden when he, by talking with Eve in Genesis 3, caused her to perceive that what God said was not good for them was in fact "good" for them after all. He knows that our perception is what will cause us to make decisions in our lives that can hinder us and cause us to be stagnant.

Our perception can either cause us to thrive or starve in the spirit as well as in the natural. When we believe and act on what the word of God says, we thrive. When we thrive, we grow, develop, prosper and flourish in our spirit man and our natural man. His word is life and strength for the believer. When we believe what situations and circumstances say, we starve our spirit man. Neglecting to feed our spirit man leaves our mind un-renewed and conformed to worldly principles, also, the body can be affected with different types of sickness and disease that are triggered by stress and depression. On any given day, our flesh is weak to fighting off temptations and unhealthy habits brought on by wrong perception, which is why we have to build up our spirit man so that he can be the most dominate of the two.

In chapter one, we talked about what you "believed" and how it dictated your decisions. There were six assessment questions that you answered which identified frustrations and hindrances in your life brought on by those beliefs. Now we're going to talk about where some of those beliefs came from which formed your perceptions.

The first question asked was "What do you believe you need to be complete or happy?" My answer to that question as you read, was how I believed that if I had someone to love, support and understand me I would be happy. This perception came from my childhood, where I felt I was never good enough for anyone to care enough to just simply love and be concerned about me. I didn't ask for much, I just simply wanted to "feel" special by specific individuals. There were some areas in my life from childhood going into my teenage years that followed me into adulthood, which left me feeling like I had a big hole in my heart. So my perception on wanting someone to love, support and understand me was initiated from me feeling abandoned, neglected and rejected as a child.

Thinking back on your answer for #1 ...

What could you have experienced in your past that helped you form a perception of what you thought would make you happy or complete?

____

____

____

____

____

____

The second question asked was, "What do you want to accomplish in the near future?" My answer was I wanted to do something to assist with the growth and development of others. This desire was motivated by different areas in my life in which I felt stunted and undeveloped.

My perception was that if I didn't do something to change the jacked up way of life that seemed to determine who qualifies to receive help, then others would have to go through what I did. It became a passion fueled by anger, hurt and disappointment.

I can remember back when I was a teenager, I wanted to succeed and accomplish great things so bad. But I didn't know how to achieve those dreams. From teachers (except one) to family members, no one took my hand to guide me in the direction I needed to go. I did have one teacher that made a referral to help me get a summer job and she encouraged me to go to college. I still had to figure out how to apply the advice given. I appreciated her for that, but I guess there was still only so much she could do. I never understood what I had to do to deserve anyone walking me through different processes to make sure I was going in the right direction.

When I applied for college, I sat in the admission office and looked at students whose demeanor said they didn't want to be there or it was just fun and games for them, but there was still someone sitting next to them holding their bags or telling them how to complete the application. I'm glad I figured it out, but didn't understand why I didn't deserve that support. I was a pretty good kid who didn't get into trouble and I wasn't rebellious. It seemed like all the attention went to kids that got into trouble.

The way I felt really bothered me, so one day, I shared my frustration of not having moral support with an older lady that I worked with and she said, "Baby the squeaky wheel always gets the oil." I remember crying so hard about that. I couldn't help but to ask myself, "Do I have to get in trouble and waste my life to receive help with resources that would assist me in being someone when I grew up?" I was under the impression that being obedient, doing well in school and reaching for my dreams was what I was supposed to do which would in turn cause someone to help me. Instead, I was always told how proud they were of me and how I was a good girl but it really didn't go much past that.

On my own, I had to figure out how to complete applications for college, housing, and jobs. This included how to get utilities turned on, where to find furniture and how was I going to get it in my new place. Whatever I needed, I had to be creative and make it happen. To this day, I know some women who can't figure out some of the things I had to as a teenager. I had to figure out everything on my own.

By the age of 16, by the grace of God, I was always able to have more than one source of income and I acquired my own apartment. Catching 2 to 3 metro buses and a train, I had to leave my apartment by 5:00 am every morning not making it home until after midnight. Then, would have to get up in the next few hours and do it all again, all the while maintaining my grades and participating in several extracurricular activities. I was determined I would not waste my life, whether I had support or not! I determined in my heart and mind that failure was not an option!

As I walked home after a long day of school and work, I would sometimes cry because it seemed like a good girl, trying to do well in school and work shouldn't have to do so much. A simple ride home would have been a blessing. It would have made things so much easier. I knew girls who had babies and their family, friends and even some teachers would give them rides to the doctor. Then after the doctor's appointment, they would catch the bus over their boyfriend's house… not the baby's daddy, but a new boyfriend with the bus tickets they received from someone who sympathized with them being young teenage mothers. I started to perceive that what was going on was just the way life was going to be. It aggravated and motivated me at the same time to want to help others and create resources for those in my situation.

Moving on to adulthood, as I stated earlier, I always had more than one source of income (that I had to create for myself might I add.) I am an entrepreneur by nature. There were very few times I felt the need to reach out for state assistance and sure enough, when I did, I made $1 too much to receive assistance. I knew girls who received state assistance and didn't even need it. They received housing vouchers (free rent) and food stamps and just continued to have babies. They would receive assistance with utilities and bus tickets. I thought to myself, "What do they need bus tickets for, just to take their kids to the zoo?" Here I was scraping to get back and forth to school and work.

I had helped countless people with rides, food, and money or just being by their side when they needed me, but nothing was ever important enough to get them to be there for me the same way. Disappointment followed me from childhood all the way to adulthood. So I operated in the place of pride coming to the conclusion that "I" was going to be the person that "I" wish

"I" had in my life. Experiences caused me to see life through the lenses of a person who had no one, would never have anyone to love them, and who wasn't lovable.

You wouldn't believe I hated taking pictures. I didn't think I was ugly, I just didn't believe I was beautiful. I would take pictures and afterwards, sit and stare at the picture and point out everything I thought was wrong with it. I also felt like if I died no one would notice. I just wanted to move out of town and go where I didn't know anyone. Then I would have a reason to be invisible.

I didn't understand how people who were mean and did evil things had so many friends. They seemed so happy. I came to the conclusion I would never be happy so I decided to just make others happy which would in turn make me happy. That way I didn't have to experience so much disappointment by expecting anything from people.

As you see, there were great things about me as a young lady that made it seem I had it all together, but inside I was broken. I was around a lot of people but felt completely alone. I found a way to cope, which helped me survive or so I thought…

I want you to think about your life. At what point did your answer for #2 become your outlook on life?

____

____

____

____

The Third question asked was, "Who or What do you "believe" is preventing you from accomplishing your goals?" My answer was myself. I was preventing myself from accomplishing my goals. Because I took on the responsibilities and obligations of others, I could not financially invest in my own projects. The perception that I needed to create a new reality for myself came from feeling abandoned in so many areas of my life by so many different individuals.

As you think back on your life…What happened to you that caused you to blame your answer (for #3) as the prevention of you achieving your goals?

____

____

____

____

The Fourth question was, "How did 'who' or 'what' become a hindrance to you accomplishing your goals?" My answer was, once again myself. I took on false assignments that cost me more than I could afford emotionally, mentally, financially and spiritually. The perception that I needed to feel needed, wanted, and accepted in order to feel a sense of worth was the problem.

Let's look at your answer (for #4), what was your perception in the area of which you allowed the hindrance to come? (Your perception is what drove you to make the decision or come to the conclusion to allow the hindrance.)

____

____

____

____

I need you to understand, what you experienced was real. You were not hallucinating. You were not crazy and it was not your fault! Satan took those situations to create a false reality for you in hopes that you would never learn the truth. The truth can only come through God's word and by being in communion with the Holy Spirit. This is the only way you will be able to heal and forgive. The truth of God's word says that you are an overcomer when satan says you are a victim. The truth of God's word says that you are victorious, when satan says you are a loser.

The word of God says that God loved you so much that He gave His only Son for you when satan says no one will ever love you. It is only when we become students of the word that we will learn who God says we are and build our perception from that truth.

The goal for this chapter, is to have you step back and evaluate your decisions, motives and intentions. Many of us had great intentions, innocent motives and made honest mistakes. We were not thinking about ourselves at the time we made our decisions. The fact is, we connected with the other person's hurt or referred to that house, car or job as a solution based on what we lacked. Our perception was off. I want you to see what we perceived our necessities were, was actually us functioning out of our hurts and pains. We crave for what we feel we need. We fight to have what we want. But God has the perfect plan for our lives if we allow Him to lead and guide us. This will minimize so many mistakes and bad decisions and in turn, give us a more peaceful, happy and prosperous life.

Prayer

Father, in the name of Jesus,

I thank You that by the truth of Your word and the guidance of Your Spirit through this chapter, I now see that my perception of things in my life has been off. I now renounce every false and lying spirit that has entered into my soulish man and caused me to make wrong decisions, emotional choices, and make unholy alliances. I now receive my deliverance through Your Spirit and I will allow You to show me who I am in You in Jesus' name.

Amen

3

“PURPOSE IS POWER”

YOU WERE PREDESTINED FOR GREATNESS!!!

Chapter 3

"But I have raised you up for this very purpose, that I might show you my power and that my name might be proclaimed in all the earth"

- Exodus 9:16

Now that we've learned the truth concerning how we believed and why we perceived things the way we did that were not healthy, it's time to be built up and move forward!

All of us were born with purpose. We have to keep in mind that nothing or no one, except us, can stop the purpose and plans of our Almighty God concerning us! At the end of the day, God will get the glory no matter what! Let's look at what God has to say about you in scripture:

Isaiah 46: 8-11 (MSG) says:*"Think about this. Wrap your minds around it. This is serious business, rebels. Take it to heart. Remember your history your long and rich history. I am God, the only God you've had or ever will have—incomparable, irreplaceable—From the very beginning telling you what the ending will be, All along letting you in on what is going to happen, Assuring you, 'I'm in this for the long haul. I'll do exactly what I set out to do,' Calling that eagle, Cyrus, out of the east, from a far country the man I chose to help me. I've said it, and I'll most certainly do it. I've planned it, so it's as good as done."*

Wow! This is so powerful! The Lord God is telling you that He knows your end from your beginning. It really doesn't matter who does what in our lives or who did what to us in our past. God has placed greatness on the inside of us that can't be done away with unless we choose not to do anything with it. We must believe the word of God when He tells us that what He has spoken concerning us, will indeed come to pass!

We must take on the attitude of Job when he said *"I know that you can do all things; no purpose of yours can be thwarted"* (Job 42:2).

When God established His purpose for our lives, it was established on purpose, because He's a God of purpose. It doesn't matter who or what throws us a curve ball, sets traps or tries to shut us down in life, God will accomplish what He started in us even if we unintentionally are part of the problem. We must know that all things work together for our good (Romans 8:28). Even the not so good stuff!

God purposed for us to live healthy and prosperous lives. This includes not just tangible things but every area of our lives.

I want to make sure that you don't allow the enemy to trick you into believing that you've waited too long or made too many mistakes for the purposes that God has concerning you to come to pass. All you have to do now is purpose in your heart to put His plans before yours and be diligent to accomplish His purposes for your life above your own. One of the worst things we can do is continue to feel like what we desire to do is more important than what He desires for us.

"Many are the plans in a person's heart, but it is the Lord's purpose that prevails" (Proverbs 19:21). It's funny how we have the audacity to make our own plans and set out to see them accomplished, but if we fail to pray and seek God's direction, we will find ourselves in a world of trouble every time. Every plan should start and finish with our hearts purposed on obeying the voice of God!

God's purpose has to always be first and foremost in our lives. We must be careful not to be fooled by great opportunities such as employment, relationships etc., because it may not fit in God's purpose or plans. This takes wisdom and maturity for us to wait on God before making emotional or hasty decisions that may have lifetime consequences. We must seek and trust Him rather than our feelings or pressures from other people.

I need you to understand that you were created on purpose with a purpose. Even though your strengths have been used as a weakness, God invested them in you because He wants to get glory out of your life in those areas. I'm going to help you focus on what your calling is, so you can be and function in the capacity that God intended!

<u>Purpose:</u> the reason for which something is done or created or for which something exists.

God in His infinite wisdom was strategic with all His creation. Everything that He made had one common purpose and that is to worship Him.

***Worship:* to honor with extravagant love and extreme submission (Webster's Dictionary, 1828).**

I'm not talking about worship from the standpoint of your favorite song or your normally scheduled church service. I'm talking about a lifestyle of holiness and discipline. This life style is driven to only please God. You are fully aware that He is in control, so you don't ever try to negotiate with Him concerning His instructions and commands.

I never understand how so many people who claim to be servants of God, have the nerve to give Him, our Creator, Redeemer, Provider, in all of His Sovereignty, all of these stipulations and ultimatums on when and how they will allow Him to use them.

When we determine what we will and will not do concerning ministry that's exactly what we're doing. I want to make clear what I'm talking about. If you have the gift to sing and you know you are anointed but say, "I don't sing in public" or you have the gift of serving but say, "I don't like dealing with people." This is a prime example of putting stipulations on the use of your gift.

Now I agree we have to use wisdom and seek God on what we do, but I still believe you must do as He instructs and not what satisfies you. The word of God says that "*To obey is better than sacrifice,*" (1Sam 15:22).
So to focus on the calling that God has placed

on your life, you have to recognize that it is He who called you to it and make sure you get your instructions from Him. Many times we go through unnecessary bumps and bruises in our walk because we claim we are "suffering for the cause of Christ" when the fact of the matter is that we have stepped out ahead of God and His guidance by the Holy Spirit and we are getting our behinds whipped by the enemy who knows we just took on the role of a rebel!

Rebel: ***a person who resists any authority, control, or tradition.***

Here is where you need to learn how satan comes in and uses your ignorance against you. When you have experienced something hurtful in your past, that most of the time God didn't tell you to do in the first place, you operated outside of His grace, which left you exposed to the enemy. Then it produced bad fruit and caused you grief, so now you say "I don't deal with people" when it's a new group of people sent by God for you to minister to. So now, because of the call on your life, if satan can get you to operate from a spirit of offence, then he has hardened your heart resulting in you not being able to be sensitive to the voice of God.

Listen, one thing we must never forget is that purpose is power and the enemy knows it! Why do you think he fights us so hard when it comes to hindering our purpose? Well here's a little insight…

Satan at one time had a purpose as well, but he allowed pride to enter his heart and it cost him big time! Look at this in Ezekiel 28:14-15, *"You were the anointed cherub who covers; I established you; You were on the holy mountain of God; you walked back and forth in the midst of fiery stones. You were perfect in your ways from the day you were created, till iniquity was found in you."*

His name was Lucifer then and he had a purpose to serve God from the day he was created as a cherub. But he came to a place where he believed he should be above the almighty God Himself! Here's another account of it in Isaiah 14:13-14, "*For you have said in your heart: 'I will ascend into heaven, I will exalt my throne above the stars of God; I will also sit on the mount of the congregation on the farthest sides of the north; I will ascend above the heights of the clouds, I will be like the Most High."*

After this, he was kicked out of heaven with no chance of redemption and it has left him angry ever since. This is why he hates the fact that we have been created with purpose and since he messed up his chance, he strongly desires to hinder us in ours. This is all the more reason why we have to be wise to his devises and more importantly, seek God for direction concerning how and when to use the gifts, talents and anointing He has placed in our lives. When we cooperate with God concerning our purpose in the earth, it is a recipe of power at its best! We get to experience the fullness of God on so many levels when it comes down to the souls of man. He loves so much carrying out the will and purpose He has placed in us. It all works in divine harmony. This is why we must understand that the things we have been predestined to do and to be have been placed on the inside of us and will only ignite when we allow God by His Spirit to navigate us through the divine path He has laid out for us. However, at the same time, if we allow the enemy to misguide us by our emotions and feelings it will cause those things to lie dormant in us and keep us feeling frustrated and unfulfilled.

At this point, we have exposed some of the tactics used by the enemy to keep us at an unhealthy place and stagnant. But thank God He has given us His word to build us up and to give us the necessary nutrients to grow and mature in Him.

In further efforts to support you on your journey, here are some scriptures to further help you view how God sees you and to show you just how much greatness is really on the inside of you.

"To them God willed to make known what are the riches of the glory of this mystery among the Gentiles: which is Christ in you, the hope of glory" (Colossians 1:27).

"For God has not given us a spirit of fear, but of power and love and of a sound mind" (2 Timothy 1:7).

"...as His divine power has given to us all things that pertain to life and godliness, through the knowledge of Him who called us by glory and virtue" (2 Peter 1:3)

Will you allow God to lead and guide you and to fulfill His purpose as He wills through your ministry?

Prayer

Father in the name of Jesus,

I repent for not making your will first priority in my life. I am sorry for not acknowledging you before making certain decisions in my life and going ahead of you as if I had the perfect plan for myself. Father it is You, who has my purpose and destiny in Your hand and I totally surrender to Your perfect will for my life. I now believe according to Your word that all that I need to accomplish Your desires for my life are already inside of me awaiting Your direction and instructions as I seek you first in Jesus name

Amen.

4

"EMBRACE WHO YOU ARE"

YOU ALREADY POSSESS EVERYTHING YOU NEED

Chapter 4

What do you believe you have been called to do? I'm not talking about what somebody told you, I'm talking about what you know in your own heart and spirit you've been called to do. If you don't know, don't be ashamed, because you are on the right track to finding out what that calling is.

Being that each of us are born with a unique purpose and calling, we must do our due diligence in finding out what our true calling is. Direction from the Holy Spirt is the only way to your discovery.

"Therefore, my dear friends, as you have always obeyed, not only in my presence, but now much more in my absence; continue to work out your salvation with fear and trembling, for it is God who works in you to will and to act in order to fulfill His good purpose" (Philippians 2:12-13).

Later in this chapter, I have listed some scriptures for you to study, meditate on, and embrace. As you are built up in your faith by the word of God, you will gain a closer relationship with the God Head (Father, Son and Holy Spirt). You will realize you are not alone and that you can do all things through Christ who strengthens you! There are a few prerequisites that we will cover, but by no means am I saying that these are the only prerequisites, but they are some that to me are very necessary.

Believe you are called:

We have to consider that who we are goes beyond who our parents and grandparents are. Jeremiah 1:5 (NIV) says *"Before I formed you in the womb I knew you, before you were born I set you apart"*... You must understand that you came from God Himself and He KNOWS you! We also can go back to creation in Genesis 1:26-27 which says: "*God said, Let Us [Father, Son, and Holy Spirit] make mankind in Our image, after Our likeness, and let them have complete authority over the fish of the sea, the birds of the air, the [tame] beasts, and over all of the earth, and over everything that creeps upon the earth. So God created man in His own image, in the image and likeness of God He created him; male and female He created them." (AMP)*

We are spirit beings who possess a body and soul. Worldly principles teach us that we are only human. According to 1 Thessalonians 5:23 we are *1/3 spirit, 1/3 body and 1/3 soul.* My husband, who is my Pastor, explains them as departments. The department that we feed the most is going to be the most dominate. In most cases, our spirit man is always the weakest of the three because most of us are ruled by our emotions, which is our soul man. He is normally the strongest out of the three. Our soul is where our passions and desires dwell and are carried out through our bodies. This is the place the enemy likes to take control of which will result in you being in bondage. He knows he can't touch your spirit man and that's why he works so hard to make sure you never learn how to build up your spirit man. Your spirit man is where the Holy Spirit dwells.

The reality is, our spirit man was given dominion. Not our soul and formed body (Genesis 2:7). Our main "DNA" originated from the Godhead (Father, Son and Holy Spirit) in Genesis 1:26. Here is where our gifts and talents were imparted in us according to His purpose and plans. God knew which family to birth us through because He knew what the bloodline consisted of. You were not a mistake, even if it seems like you are the odd-ball or black sheep in your family. Even if you come from a dysfunctional family, God knew exactly what He was doing.

You have to keep in mind that you are the "chosen one." Matthew 22:14 says *"For many are called, but few are chosen."*

Let's consider David…

He comes from a large family of brave shepherds and musicians. In result, as a child, he defeated Goliath and was a gifted musician. He along with his family was considered to be a good-looking family. David was obedient to his father and named an honorable young man. This didn't mean everything was perfect for him. He had a brother named Eliab who always gave him a hard time for no reason. At the age of 15 he was anointed king by the instructions of the Lord. This caused his brothers to really resent him.

David was a man with many issues and yet was still referred to by God Himself as "a man after God's own heart."

This is a perfect example of God knowing what family you needed to be birth through by the gifts and talents that he invested in your families' bloodline. Every quality David had as a child, enabled him to be the warrior and king he truly was. In spite of him being a murderer, bad father, and adulterer…God had purpose for his life.

Through his bloodline, David like his great-grandmother Ruth, would display great courage in various situations. Ruth a Moabitess, was going to ask Boaz, a Jew, to marry her at the request of her mother-in-law Naomi, even though she could have been reproached as an immodest woman for doing so or even despised as a poor woman. As a result, she would bear a son who would bring forth Israel's most famous king: David. This was all a part of God's divine plan. David going before Goliath on behalf of the people of Israel to challenge him and ultimately slay him, was also a part of God's purpose.

Though David displayed similar strengths from his bloodline, it did not stop him from making wrong, emotional and sometimes very mean decisions. However, God, having the ability to see man's heart, still used him greatly. Just like David, we may have made some stupid decisions in the past but God still has purpose for us. God will not take away what He placed in you no more than He took the anointing away from David as king. So whether you came to the conclusion on your own or satan lied and told you that you are unusable, the truth is that the anointing inside of you is being activated even as you read this book. Purpose in your heart to obey God!

As it comes down to the purpose and plan of God for our lives, we now have a better covenant with God than David had. We unlike David, are now merged together with God the Father by a more precious blood line than David and that is the blood of Jesus Christ! You must understand, that if the blood of Jesus was not shed for you, you would not have been a recipient of the purpose of God. So the power is in you believing that you are called, justified and qualified by God!

Now, as we focus our attention on what He has called us to do, He will continue to complete the work that He has begun in us which will enable us to be effective in our calling.

In spite of your past, what do you find yourself doing or desiring to do on a regular basis? Something you find yourself doing like a reflex. It doesn't require thought, you just automatically find yourself doing it. You are good at it and it's all you think about doing.

What is it?

____

____

____

____

These scriptures express the *intentions* of God concerning your calling:

For we are His workmanship, created in Christ Jesus for good works, which God prepared beforehand so that we would walk in them (Ephesians 2:20).

You did not choose Me but I chose you, and appointed you that you would go and bear fruit, and that your fruit would remain, so that whatever you ask of the Father in My name He may give to you (John 15:16).

And these whom He predestined, He also called; and these whom He called, He also justified; and these whom He justified, He also glorified (Romans 8:30).

Therefore, brethren, be all the more diligent to make certain about His calling and choosing you; for as long as you practice these things, you will never stumble; (2 Peter 1:10).

Trust God with you:

Trusting God with you is one of the most important pieces of this whole puzzle. To trust God is to believe on His word and to believe on His word is to do as His word says.

I've learned trusting requires discipline. It's something how when God is telling you to do something, most of the time you don't see how what He wants you to do is even possible. Be it finances, the help of others, being received from others, or knowledge to do what He has called you to do. You must trust that His grace is going to allow you to accomplish what He intended. I have learned there is always provision for the vision and our only part is to commit to the vision.

I want you to see where discipline is required in trusting God. God may tell you to make a specific phone call to someone you may not want to call. Discipline enables you to be obedient and make the call anyway. In another instance, you may get instructions on doing something that could make you look totally crazy to people. Your obedience gives you courage and it overrides your fears and doubts.

This is a serious issue in the body of Christ. The fear of God has left the church somehow and people think they can do what they want, when they want, and how they want.

We must obey the voice of God. To obey the voice of God one must know how to recognize the voice of God. Luke 11:28 says *"Blessed rather are those who hear the word of God and obey it."* It also says in James 1:25, *"But he who looks into the perfect law of liberty and continues in it, and is not a forgetful hearer but a doer of the work, this one will be blessed in what he does."*

Everything that we need has already been given to us to be and do everything God intended.

2 Peter 1:3 says, *"His divine power has given us everything we need for a godly life through our knowledge of him who called us by his own glory and goodness."*

Let's talk about Joseph, the son of Jacob whose name was changed to Israel. Joseph lived a life completely depended on God. No matter what adversity he faced, he continued to entrust his life in the hands of God.

This can be found in the account of when Joseph was falsely accused and put in jail. During that time, the chief butler and chief baker offended their lord, the king of Egypt, who threw them in jail with Joseph (Gen 40:1-7). Both, the butler and baker had dreams, but had no one to interpret them. Joseph said *"Do not interpretations belong to God? Tell them, I pray you"* (Gen 40:8).

God gave Joseph the interpretations, and both came to pass. The butler kept his job, and the baker lost his life. You would think that the butler would have been anxious to tell others what happened. Nope!

He said nothing for two years. This is where a lot of us would get in our feelings and either tell people what God used us to do or stop talking to the person that we helped, because they didn't recognize what we had done.

That wasn't the response of Joseph. He knew the plan and purpose of God would be fulfilled in his life and would come to pass. Sure enough, opportunity presented itself, Pharaoh had a dream that all the magicians of Egypt could not interpret. God was about to set up a grand entrance for Joseph. The king learned of Joseph's ability to interpret dreams, he sent for him and asked if he could interpret his dream. You better know, Joseph was ready! He confidently answered in Genesis 41:16 saying, *"It is not in me: God shall give Pharaoh an answer of peace."*

By the Spirit of God, Joseph interpreted Pharaoh's dream. The king could do nothing but recognize the Spirit of God upon Joseph. He responded by saying in (Gen. 41:39-40), *"Forasmuch as God hath shewed thee all this, there is none as discreet and wise as thou art: Thou shalt be over my house, and according unto thy word shall all my people be ruled: only in the throne will I be greater than thou."*

A promotion and platform like that can only come for our faithful, loving, and Almighty God! Please allow courage to fill your heart and spirit right now in the name of Jesus. God is calling you to greater, although your current situations may not feel so great, BUT GOD!

Everything we are experiencing, while birthing the visions God is calling us to release at this appointed time, has a due season if we refuse to give up. Galatians 6:9 says, *"And let us not be weary in well doing: for in due season we shall reap, if we faint not."*

Before you answer the next question, I want to make something clear. Any idea, invention, desire, or dream you have comes from the heart and mind of God. It doesn't have to be something that is used per say in a church building. It can be a catering company, transportation company, book, blog, newsletter, boutique, band, cleaning service, etc…What happens is, because you are part of establishing His Kingdom, He entrusted you with the assignment to govern the tool He wants to use for His Glory.

The importance of you moving on what has been assigned to you is because you may be responsible for employing His people giving them a safe environment to work with the perfect schedule and pay. You may be the one to clean someone's home because you and your anointing is what's keeping the death angel away or any satanic attack. You could be the one who is responsible for His purpose fulfilled through what He has given you to do. You must know, there is always a bigger picture.

I want to end this with a few thoughts to ponder. Who is praying for God to send them a blessing that rests in your hands? Are you available to be part of what God wants to accomplish? Think about the job you prayed for. If someone didn't start the company, how would that have affected you? What if all your prayers concerning things were held up because the person responsible for creating, producing or starting it was too afraid, too busy, too stressed out to step out and bring their dreams to life. You would be in a jacked up situation. Let's walk in love and say yes to God and help establish His Kingdom!

What instructions have God given you, that for whatever reason, you haven't followed concerning your God-given assignment?

____

____

____

____

____

____

____

____

These scriptures <u>*assure*</u> you that God is with you and for you!

"When he puts forth all his own, he goes ahead of them, and the sheep follow him because they know his voice."(John 10:4)

"For I know the plans I have for you, declares the Lord, plans for welfare and not for evil, to give you a future and a hope." (Jeremiah 29:11)

"Fear not, for I am with you; be not dismayed, for I am your God; I will strengthen you, I will help you, I will uphold you with my righteous right hand." (Isaiah 41:10).

"Be strong. Take courage. Don't be intimidated. Don't give them a second thought because God, your God, is striding ahead of you. He's right there with you. He won't let you down; he won't leave you." (Deuteronomy 31:6) {MSG}

<u>Pray for direction:</u>

If you keep in mind that your number one responsibility is to obey God, thank Him for favor and resources to accomplish what He has called you to do, then He can fulfill His obligation of bringing the vision to pass. I think we sometimes lose sight of the fact, that if God tells us to do something that He has the ultimate plan and strategy. We somehow focus on how we are going to make it happen only to find ourselves doing nothing in the end. God may not give you all the instructions at first, but you have to just make a move on what he gave you in the beginning.

I know we have been taught that God is in control of everything, however, there is a part we have to do in order for the purpose and plan of God for our lives to come to fruition. He isn't going to do everything for us, if He were, why then would He leave us

His Spirit who He said in John 16 will lead and guide us into all truth. We should be making phone calls, doing research on the Internet, and networking as the Holy Spirit leads and He will let us know exactly what decisions to make. Here is where we allow fear to creep in because we don't want to make any mistakes.

I once heard a great man of God say, "If you aim at nothing you will hit it every time!" When we go in Jesus' name we must walk in expectation. We can't prejudge or put God in a box in determining how or what He chooses to use to bless us. 1 Corinthians 1:27 says, *"But God hath chosen the foolish things of the world to confound the wise; and God hath chosen the weak things of the world to confound the things which are mighty."*

When praying for direction, keep your preferences out of the equation. Allow God to do as He pleases and I assure you it will be the smartest thing you will ever do! First of all, you will have peace, you won't have to compromise with your integrity, God will always make provision for the vision, and you will see the manifestations of God's glory upon your endeavor.

This place is different from settling for less. When you settle, you experience fear or anxiousness because you feel pressured to make a decision in fear of losing or missing out. If God requires you to make a quick decision, you will have peace and not anxiety. Anxiety cannot operate when confidence or certainty is functioning. According to Psalm 37:23, *"The steps of a good man are ordered by the Lord: and he delighteth in his way."* He will lead and guide you if you finish the race.

Don't allow discouragement through people not supporting you stop you. Jesus was not supported in His own town (Luke 4:14-30). What if He gave up after being rejected by the people He felt should have supported Him, but they didn't? You and I would be in a world of trouble.

I just want to "*inCourage*" you to stay focused on what God has called you to do and follow instructions. Know that He is with you every step of the way!

Next are a few scriptures of the Lord's <u>promises</u> to give us guidance and direction when we turn to Him:

"Thus says the Lord, your Redeemer, the Holy One of Israel: "I am the Lord your God, who teaches you to profit, who leads you by the way you should go" (Isaiah 48:17).

"I will instruct you and teach you in the way you should go; I will guide you with My eye" (Psalm 32:8).

"Trust in the Lord with all your heart, and lean not on your own understanding; in all your ways acknowledge Him, and He shall direct your paths" (Proverbs 3:5).

Answer the call:

You are the only one who can determine if you are truly called. The confession of your faith and conviction of your heart produces evidence through your lifestyle, which allows the power of God to flow through your calling. No matter what the calling is, you are responsible to make sure you exemplify Christ to the best of your ability by the help of God. Your goal must be to allow your life to represent what you say you believe concerning the word of God.

I have listed here both the Amplified version as well as the New King James version of Romans 12:1: *"Therefore I urge you, brothers and sisters, by the mercies of God, to present your bodies [dedicating all of yourselves, set apart] as a living sacrifice, holy and well-pleasing to God, which is your rational (logical, intelligent) act of worship."* (NKJV) *"I beseech you therefore, brethren, by the mercies of God, that you present your bodies a living sacrifice, holy, acceptable to God, which is your reasonable service."*

Answering the call doesn't mean you have it all together. It clearly requires you to become a student of the word. This allows your life to come into alignment with the word of God, as you mature in your ministry. You will constantly be learning and growing until the return of Jesus Christ. God knows you don't know everything, that's why a healthy relationship with the Holy Spirit is so key. 2 Corinthians 13:14 tells us that our fellowship should be with the Holy Spirit. He is the one that will reveal the mysteries of God to you. You do your part and let God do the rest.

Hebrews 11:1 says *"faith is being sure of what we hope for and certain of what we do not see."* When God calls you, you must respond by faith. Faith is total trust and dependence on God! Everything we do is activated by faith. James 2:17 says, *"Faith by itself, if it is not accompanied by action, is dead."*

God has equipped you with everything you will ever need to successfully do what He has called you to do.

<u>Commit to your calling:</u>

Jesus said in Luke 9:62, *"no one who puts his hand to the plow and looks back is fit for service in the kingdom of God."* Once you answer the call of God, you can't turn back!

When you answer the call of God, you have to govern yourself according to your call. There are specific requirements to every call. Those requirements could include, but are not limited to:

- ✓ Special diet, if God deals with you in dreams.
- ✓ Organizational skills if you are a business owner.
- ✓ Strong prayer life if you are an intercessor or prophet.

These are all examples of your lifestyle being the incubator that protects and nurtures your anointing. You must be mindful of your environments, what you use to entertain yourself, who you keep company with, etc. This brings an awareness that you can operate in power at any given point. Being at the gas station, grocery store, mall or wherever. You are always prepared!

Whether good, bad, or indifferent, you should never neglect your calling. A commitment should stand no matter what comes or goes. You have to keep in mind that you are not called by man, but by God Himself. Regardless of what people say, do or fail to do, you have accepted the policies and procedures of your calling. I'm referring to whatever it takes for you to be effective. This brings to mind the word diligent. The more diligent you are, the more knowledgeable you become by studying and through hands-on application.

Let's take a police officer for example. An off-duty cop, out of his suit, is an average Joe. In his suit, he is backed by the authority of the law. Police go through strenuous training to obtain their office. They are expected to know and uphold the law. Here is where good cops and bad cops are identified. A good cop can have an encounter with a non-compliant and combative individual, but because he knows his authority, he deals with it according to the policy and procedures of the constitution and not compromise his integrity by allowing his emotions to take control. The bad cop disregards the policy and procedures and takes things into his own hands by allowing his ego and emotions to take control and now he acts in violation of what he committed to, which was to protect and serve.

When you commit to your calling, you are willing to do whatever it takes to be effective in that area at all cost. You invest your money and time into what you have been called to do. You sacrifice your pleasures to please God. You sacrifice relationships that conflict with your calling. Your loyalty is to God and that's that!

I want you to understand, you must be knowledgeable of what is required to function in your calling as well as what character and lifestyle practices are required. This is where different trainings, workshops, and one on one's with your leaders, teachers or mentors come into play. All of this, along with your personal time with the Holy Spirt, will make you a force to be reckoned with! Below I have listed a few things for you to think about. Some of them you may or may not have done already, but hopefully it helps you with sorting out your thoughts as you position yourself for greatness!

What is the purpose of the ministry or service you want to provide?

____

____

____

____

Who is your targeted audience?

____

What needs if any, will your ministry or company seek to meet?

How will your ministry or company meet those needs?

How will you market or promote your services?

<u>Other Things to Consider (not limited to)</u>

* ***Networking with ministries or companies that are the same as yours***

* ***Find a knowledgeable mentor or advisor***

* ***Make sure you always have business cards***

* ***Educate yourself in the area in which you want to serve:***

    - ***Dos and Don'ts***
    - ***Strategies and Tips***
    - ***Proper Credentials (If applicable)***

* ***Where will you provide your services***

* ***Take advantage of social media***

* ***Get proper registrations and licenses***

* ***Consider how much does it cost to run your ministry or business***

Prayer

Father God in the name of Jesus,

I thank you for loving me for me. I thank you for seeing the best in me when I didn't have a mind to be my best. Father be pleased with me. My only desire is to be pleasing in your sight. Father I trust you with me and I believe your word concerning me. I am so grateful to serve a true and living God that is so faithful, loving and merciful. Father I Give all of me to do as you will.

In Jesus' name Amen!

5

"YOU IN FULL EFFECT"

ALLOWING HIS GLORY TO BE REVEALED

Conclusion

Today you operate with a new grace that allows you the opportunity to flow in your calling like never before. As you implement the changes that have been revealed to you through the Holy Spirit, I pray your confidence in God becomes immeasurable. This new season of your life requires some repositioning.

Just like you can rearrange your furniture and create a totally different ambiance in a room, you have been afforded the opportunity to rearrange and reposition your life. God wants you to see that by trusting Him, you are now able to flow in the supernatural realm. Now that your faith has grown, your sensitivity to the Holy Spirit is keener, you are free to operate in your anointing. I encourage you to continue to invest in who you are, because you are your greatest investment! Make consistent deposits in your knowledge of God and our Lord and Savior Jesus Christ. Make continual withdrawals from your faith.

I feel the need to give you a heads up. Satan is not going to just step to the side and allow this to be easy for you. For every level there is a new devil…

But I'm excited to say there is also a new grace. When we stand for God we become targets of opposition and adversity. But we have to stay focused and remember *"For we do not wrestle against flesh and blood, but against principalities, against powers, against the rulers of the darkness of this age, against spiritual hosts of wickedness in the heavenly places"* (Ephesians 6:12).

By keeping this in mind, we can continue to love those that yield themselves to the devil. And we can forgive and release those that hurt us. This place allows us to respond –vs- react to situations and circumstances. Now we are walking in His glory and not our story!

I want to warn you! This new you will not be accepted by everyone especially those closest to you. Your faith and integrity will be tried, but you have to stand your ground with the enemy. God will allow you to see the traps and plots from a mile away. He will allow you to smell smoke ahead of time when the enemy tries to smoke you out. You will be enabled to make wise decisions rather than emotional decisions because you are God centered and focused.

I'm excited for your ministry and or business because I know if God is allowed to be God, you are going to soar higher than an eagle.

I want to reiterate, stay focused! Whatever God shows you, take heed and follow instructions. Have an open mind and spirit concerning your partnership with Him. Be careful not to box Him in or go ahead of Him. He knows the end from the beginning, so allow Him to do what He does and that is Be God!

Blessings I leave with you! Go and grow in the things of God and see the salvation of the Lord!

Grace and Peace.

Prophetic Declarations

I decree and declare that in the name of Jesus...

Your ministry will flourish

Your business will flourish

Open access to resources and finances

Creative abilities and witty inventions

The Favor of God with everything concerning you

Peace of mind

A hostile free atmosphere in your home, office and ministry

All barriers, boundaries and hindrances be destroyed

Mental and emotional stability

Freedom from all satanic and demonic strongholds, bondages, entrapments, manipulations, past hurts, disappointments, fear, timidity, and insecurities

You shall be of good courage

You shall operate in boldness

You shall run and not be weary

You shall walk and not faint

You shall do the will of the Father in liberty

Your name will be known among great men and women of God

You are the salt of the earth

You are an ambassador of God

You will be instrumental in the building up of God's Kingdom and the destroying of satan's kingdom

Your ministry or business will help advance the agenda of our Father

You arc loved

You are worth it

You are important

You are needed

You are "inCourage"

I love you with all my heart. I need you to know I believe in you and what God has invested in you! You are not alone in this journey. All of my contact info can be found on my website arlethakentministries.org. Feel free to reach out to me anytime. I will keep you in my prayers.

God said it! That settled it! Now you just need to believe it! Be strong in the Lord and in the power of His might. And remember...

You are Backed by God, Endorsed by Jesus Christ, and Managed by the Holy Spirit!

Notes

Notes

Notes

Notes

Notes

Notes

Notes

Notes

Notes

Notes

References

http://dictionary.reference.com
http://www.merriam-webster.com
https://www.kingjamesbibleonline.org
https://www.biblegateway.com

About Prophetess Arletha Kent

As His workmanship, my worship is being perfected, allowing His purpose to be fulfilled in my life for His glory." (Ephesians 2:10)

Backed by God, Endorsed by Jesus Christ, and Managed by the Holy Spirit!

Arletha S. Kent, a native of St. Louis, MO, is the wife of 15 years to Pastor Travis C. Kent Jr.

In October 2013, she along with her husband answered the call to establish and pastor True Image Empowerment Outreach Ministries where they serve at this present time.

Co-Pastor Arletha Kent has been serving in the Lord's ministry for over 15 years. She is an Ordained Prophetess, a Watchman, a Spiritual Midwife and Life Coach that God has entrusted with one of His deliverance ministries.

Her gifts and talents are numerous to say the least. She is a High Impact Motivational Speaker, Author, Play Writer, Director, and Entrepreneur.

Currently, Arletha is a published author, her first book entitled *inCourage: Strengthened From Within.* She has a jewelry business called "Heartense Fashions Unlimited" where she provides not only jewelry, but beauty services, customized clothing and fragrances as well.

Prophetess Kent is on a mission to fulfill her divine assignment given by God to destroy the works of the devil. She operates under a heavy prophetic anointing and her discernment is with pin-point accuracy. As a Prophet, Watchman and Spiritual Midwife, God has given her a no nonsense position concerning the tactics, devices, schemes and plots of the enemy, which allows the Holy Spirit to heal, deliver, and set the captives free. Through the ministry gifts of Prophetess Kent, the believer is able to give birth to their ministry and grow and develop into their God-given calling. She has counseled countless men, women and children leading them into their deliverance and breakthrough.

Lady Kent continues to use her gifts as a beacon of light and encouragement to those struggling with their walk with God and as a sign of hope and witness to a dying world that Jesus not only saves, but heals, delivers and sets the captives free!

www.arlethakentministries.org

True Image Empowerment Outreach Ministries

If you are looking for a word from the Lord, True Image Empowerment Outreach Ministries Invites you to join us! Currently, we fellowship inside of the Dellwood Recreation Center located at 10266 West Florissant 63136. Come with expectation!!! Below is our contact info. If you have any questions or would like to reach out to us!

Service Times:
Sunday: 1pm-3pm
Tuesday: 7pm – 8:30pm

Contact Info:
Phone: 314-328-9915
Email: tieom.new1@yahoo.com
Facebook: www.facebook.com/T.I.Ministries
Website: tieom.org

Heartense Fashions Unlimited LLC.
Founder/CEO: Arletha S. Kent

Heartense Fashions Unlimited LLC. Provides a wide range of accessories including customized jewelry, fragrance oils and women's clothing. Our clothing caters to the woman with imperfections who is tired of running from store to store to find something that compliments her body regardless of size. All of our items will focus on camouflaging problem areas, be it top-heavy, muffin tops, large midsection, baby pooch, etc.

If you are interested in more information including upcoming events featuring Heartense Fashions Unlimited, please email arlethakent@yahoo.com.